FREE DIVING

To my mother, Charlotte,
for giving me life to pursue my dreams
LC

For my legendary support crew Scotty,
Summer, Benny, Jesse and Olly
BH

First published 2017, reprinted 2019, 2025 x3
Magabala Books Aboriginal Corporation,
Broome, Western Australia
Website: www.magabala.com   Email: sales@magabala.com

Magabala Books receives financial assistance from the Commonwealth Government through Creative Australia, its arts advisory body. The State of Western Australia has made an investment in this project through the Department of Local Government, Sport and Cultural Industries.

Designed by Jo Hunt
Printed in China by Toppan Leefung Printing Ltd

ISBN 978-1-925360-73-8

A catalogue record for this book is available from the National Library of Australia

FREE DIVING

Lorrae Coffin

Illustrated by

Bronwyn Houston

We're heading out into the open sea,
on a lugger with a colourful crew.

Searching for that hidden pearl,
snuggled in a haven of blue.

I wave goodbye to my family,
and pray that I will return in one piece.

Diving down with no tank on my back,
just the air in my lungs to help me.

I'm a long way from home,
my country, my people I leave.

I'm free diving, into the water I go.

With a Malay man to watch my back,

and a Japanese man watching my side.

The night is warm and the moon is high,
but my body feels like ice.

The diver's arms wrap around my chest,
saying everything is all right.

I hear the seagulls scream,
and the voice of the captain
telling me to earn my keep.

I'm free diving, into the water I go.

No Malay man to watch my back,
and no Japanese man watching my side.

I'm free diving.

FREE DIVING

Lorrae Coffin © 1996

♩= 70

Am Em C D

Verse One

Am   Em
Heading out into the open sea on a lugger with a colourful crew.
Am   Em
Searching for that hidden pearl, snuggled in a haven of blue.
Am   Em
Wave goodbye to my family, pray that I will return in one piece
Am   Em
Diving down with no tank on my back, just the air in my lungs to help me.

Bridge #1

        C   D   Em   C   D   Em
I'm a long way from home. My country, my people I leave.
C   D   Em   C
I hear the seagulls scream. And the voice of the captain telling me to,
D
earn my keep.

CHORUS

           C   Em   C   Em   C   Em
So I'm ... free diving. Into the water I go. Yes I'm free diving.
C   D
A Malay man to watch my back and a Japanese man watching my side.
       Em
Free Diving.

Verse Two

The night is warm and the moon is high. But my body feels like ice.

The diver's arms wrap around my chest. Saying everything is alright.

Bridge #2

But I'm a long way from home. My country my people I leave.

I hear the seagulls scream. And the voice of the captain telling me to,

earn my keep.

CHORUS

C Em C Em C Em

So I'm ... free diving. Into the water I go. Yes I'm free diving.

C D

No Malay man to watch my back and no Japanese watching my side.

Am Am Em

Free diving.

The song *Free Diving* was written by Lorrae Coffin to remember the Indigenous men and women who worked as 'free divers' in the pearling industry in Western Australia from the mid-1800s.

In a practice known as 'blackbirding' (forced unpaid labour), European pearl lugger owners used Indigenous people to dive for pearl shell. With no protective suits, the divers faced threats such as decompression sickness known as the 'bends', shark attack or of being swept away by huge tides. At sea for weeks at a time, there was also the risk of the luggers being shipwrecked in cyclones that formed off the coast.

Free Diving is a fictionalised story of a young man lost at sea.

Lorrae Coffin is a descendant of the Nyiyaparli and Yindijibarndi people of the Pilbara in Western Australia. She is a singer–songwriter and co-founder of Marrugeku, a leader in intercultural dance theatre. Lorrae is recognised throughout Australia for her knowledge of the Indigenous arts music industry. *Free Diving* is her first book.

Bronwyn Houston grew up in Broome and finds her inspiration in the natural world. She is descended from the Wunna Nyiyaparli people of the Pilbara and her dad's family is English and Scottish. Bronwyn has written and illustrated several books including the *Return of the Dinosaurs* (Magabala Books 2016).